Art Works™ Drawing Monsters

Carolyn Scrace

A+

Smart Apple Media

Author:
Carolyn Scrace graduated from Brighton College of Art, England, after studying design and illustration. She has since worked in animation, advertising, and children's publishing. She has a special interest in natural history and has written many books on the subject, including *Lion Journal,* and *Gorilla Journal* in the *Animal Journal* series.

How to use this book:

Follow the easy, numbered instructions. Simple step-by-step stages enable budding young artists to create their own amazing drawings.

What you will need:

1. Paper.
2. Wax crayons.
3. Felt-tip pens to add color.

Published by Smart Apple Media, an imprint of Black Rabbit Books
P.O. Box 3263, Mankato, Minnesota 56002
www.blackrabbitbooks.com

Published by arrangement with
The Salariya Book Company Ltd

Cataloging-in-Publication Data is available from the Library of Congress

Printed in the United States
At Corporate Graphics,
North Mankato, Minnesota

9 8 7 6 5 4 3 2

ISBN: 978-1-62588-346-9

Contents

Sparks!

1 Sparks needs a head,

2 ...a short body with two legs,

3 ...two arms and hands,

4 ...two feet,

5 ...three big round eyes, a tiny nose, and spiky hair!

6 Now draw in his big mouth with pointed teeth.

Use crayons to add color and some monster spots all over Sparks's face, body, legs, and feet.

5

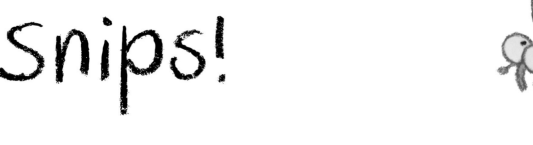

Snips!

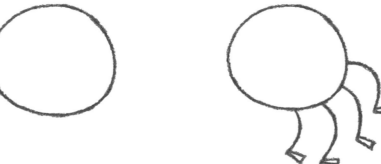

1 Snips needs a body,

2 ...four legs and feet,

3 ...and four more legs and feet!

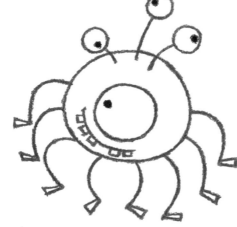

4 Now draw in one **big** eye,

5 ...a mouth and teeth,

6 ...and her three wobbly eyes on stalks!

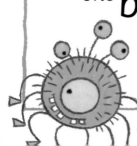

6

Draw in thin lines
to make Snips's
body hairy.

Color in with
felt-tip pens.

7

Widget!

1 Widget needs a body,

2 ...a head,

3 ...two arms and hands,

4 ...two legs and feet!

5 Now draw in two big ears and a nose,

6 ...two eyes, a mouth, and teeth!

8

Use a crayon to color the inside shape of Widget's ears.

Color in with felt-tip pens.

Add some pointy scales to Widget's body,

...and her beautiful curly tail!

9

 # Chisel!

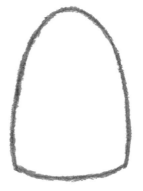

1 Chisel needs a body,

2 ...a head,

3 ...two legs and feet,

4 ...two long arms and hands,

5 ...and a **big** mouth and teeth!

6 Now draw one big eye and his tiny horns!

10

Use a white crayon to add stripes to Chisel's body.

Color in with felt-tip pens.

11

Rasp!

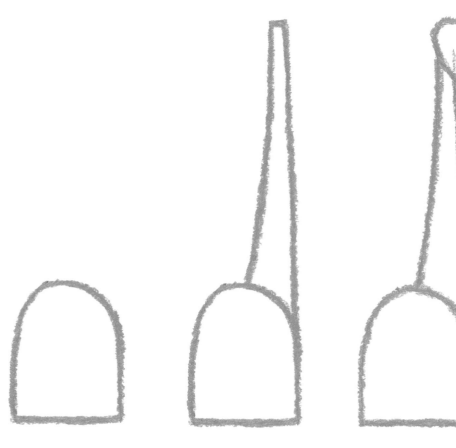

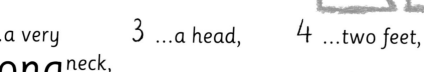

1 Rasp needs
a body,

2 ...a very
long neck,

3 ...a head,

4 ...two feet,

Horn

Draw in
a zigzag
shape all the
way down
the back of
Rasp's body.

Color in
with felt-tip
pens.

5 ...and two arms
and hands.

6 Draw in two eyes,
a horn, and his
big smile.

13

Mallet!

1 Mallet needs
a body,

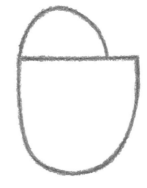

2 ...a head,

3 ...two legs and feet,

4 ...two arms
and hands,

5 ...a tail,

6 ...an eye, a nose, and
a **big** mouth!

Draw in lots of pointed teeth!

Add spots to Mallet's body and tail with a crayon.

Color in with felt-tip pens.

15

Plug!

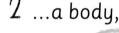

1 Plug needs a head,

2 ...a body,

3 ...three legs and feet,

4 ...and two arms and hands.

5 Now add her eyes, nose, and a big mouth,

6 ...with **lots** of teeth!

16

Horns

Draw in Plug's
two ears and two
sharp horns.

Now add spots
to her face.

Color in with
felt-tip pens.

17

Spanner!

1 Spanner needs a head,

2 ...a body,

3 ...two legs, feet, and a tail,

Stalks

4 ...and **four** arms and hands.

5 Now draw in Spanner's big eyes on stalks,

6 ...and her nose, mouth, and teeth!

Use a crayon to add spots to Spanner's face, body, and tail.

Color in with felt-tip pens.

19

Bolt!

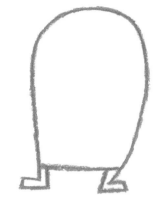

1 Bolt needs a body,

2 ...two small legs, and feet,

3 ...two big arms and hands,

4 ...a very **big** mouth and teeth!

5 Draw in two eyes, a nose,

6 ...and his two horns.

Draw in spots on Bolt's body, arms and hands, and stripes on his horns.

Color in with felt-tip pens.

21

Clamp!

1 Clamp needs a head,   2 ...a body,   3 ...two legs and feet,

4 ...two arms and
hands,

5 ...two eyes and one
long nose like an
elephant's trunk!

6 Add his mouth
and teeth.

22

Color in with
felt-tip pens.

Use a crayon
to draw stripes
on his body.

Draw in Clamp's tail.

23

  # Putty!

1 Putty needs **two** heads,

2 ...a body,

3 ...**two** necks, two legs and feet,

4 ...two arms and hands,

5 ...and **one** tail!

6 Draw a big eye on each of her heads.

Draw in Putty's mouth and teeth and add a zigzag pattern to her body and tail.

Color in with felt-tip pens.

25

Pincer!

1 Pincer needs a head,

2 ...a wiggly body,

3 ...two arms and hands,

4 ...and **lots** of legs and feet!

5 Draw in two eyes and horns,

6 ...and her long nose and teeth.

26

Draw in Pincer's antennae!

antennae

Add stripes to her horns and body using crayons.

Color in with felt-tip pens.

27

Nut!

1 Nut needs a **big** head,

2 ...a **small** body,

3 ...two legs and feet,

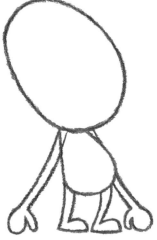

4 ...and two long arms and hands.

5 Add two big eyes, a nose, and mouth,

6 ...and two antennae!

Draw in Nut's sharp teeth and finish off his eyes.

Use crayons to add spots to Nut's head and stripes to his body.

Color in with felt-tip pens.

Sprocket!

 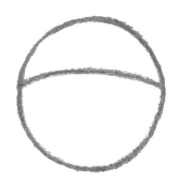 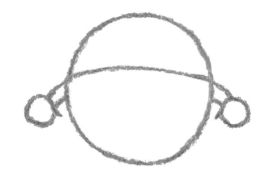

1 Sprocket needs a **fat** body,

2 ...a **huge** mouth,

3 ...two tiny arms and hands,

4 ...two legs and feet,

5 ...and two **extra** legs and feet!

6 Now draw in one eye, his teeth, and two antennae!

Color in with felt-tip pens.

31

Glossary

Antennae   stalks or feelers that grow on the heads of some animals.

Eyestalk   a movable stalk with an eye on top.

Horn   a hard, bony spike that grows out of an animal's head. Some animals use their horns to defend themselves from attack.

Scales   small, hard plates that cover and protect the bodies of some animals.

Tail   the back part of an animal that helps it balance.

Index